Dream Happy
Be Great

Written by Gary Krutz Ph. D.
Illustrated by Justin L. Walsh
Copyright 2017

This book is intended to build a better society by providing insight into treating and respecting all people. Parents and teachers can use this book with children from ages 2-11. It is suggested that you expand upon each page interactively with children about other ways the ideas presented in this book can make people happy.

Part 1

Ages 2-6

Be Happy

Enjoy yourself with friends. Tell stories, live, laugh, love, and create happy memories.

Smile Happy

Tell People:

"You are beautiful."

"You brighten my day."

"You are wonderful."

Tell your mother, father, and siblings that you love them. Say things like:

"You are terrific."

"Thank you for caring."

Teamwork

Get involved with others to achieve a common goal. You can accomplish big things by working together as a team.

Conversation

Talk to others around you. Ask them about their day. Become a happy home. Take care with electronic messages and use kind words.

Talk Happy

Kind words will help friends have a good day. Show respect for other people's opinions.

Refrain from gossiping. Stay away from bad words or saying mean words that will hurt another person's feelings.

Stealing is Bad

Never take things that do not belong to you.
Refrain from asking others to do the wrong thing.
Do not hurt or physically harm other people.

Giving is Great

Be grateful for what you have. Giving to others makes your heart happy.

Eat Well

Feel better by eating fruits, vegetables, grains, dairy, and protein. Become stronger and feel more healthy by eating a balanced diet.

Job Diversity

There are many different types of jobs. All are important and necessary for a community to function. All jobs are happy jobs.

Good Advice

Ask your parents or a teacher for advice, they will provide safe answers. Say please and thank you.

Stay happy by keeping clean. Stop germs by washing your hands.

Be Careful

Keep away from sharp objects,
which can hurt you and other people.
Look for warning labels.

Toxic Chemicals

Stay away from chemical cleaning products. Keep dangerous cleaners and liquids out of the reach of children.
Do not touch toxic chemicals!

Drugs

Resist doing drugs unless they are prescribed to you by your doctor. Stay away from illegal drugs.

Alcohol and Tobacco

Alcohol and tobacco can be hazardous to your health.

Bullying

It is not nice to put others down. Pushing can result in a fall and could hurt you or other friends.

Help Others

Helping other people makes your heart happy. Ask your parents how you can help out around the house.

Notes

How to make someone happy...

Example: Go fishing with Grandpa.

Dream Happy Be Great

Notes

Ways to help out...

Example: Plant flowers with Grandma.

Dream Happy Be Great

Notes

Talking happy...

Example: Say please and thank you.

Dream Happy *Be Great*

Made in United States
Orlando, FL
21 November 2022